Haiku PUNchlines: Giggles and Groans

Book Six

Paul Treatman

iUniverse, Inc.
Bloomington

Haiku PUNchlines: Giggles and Groans
Book Six

iUniverse books may be ordered through booksellers or by contacting:

iUniverse
1663 Liberty Drive
Bloomington, IN 47403
www.iuniverse.com
1-800-Authors (1-800-288-4677)

Because of the dynamic nature of the Internet, any web addresses or links contained in this book may have changed since publication and may no longer be valid. The views expressed in this work are solely those of the author and do not necessarily reflect the views of the publisher, and the publisher hereby disclaims any responsibility for them.

Any people depicted in stock imagery provided by Thinkstock are models, and such images are being used for illustrative purposes only.

Certain stock imagery © Thinkstock.

ISBN: 978-1-4697-7916-4 (sc)
ISBN: 978-1-4697-7917-1 (e)

Printed in the United States of America

iUniverse rev. date: 5/9/2012

Acknowledgements

Thank you, Sylvia Rubin, your love and devotion are my raison d'être.

This little volume is my latest in a sextology (is there such a word?) of six books of haikus with a twist, the twist being the embedding of a pun in the haiku text. This twisted haiku is, I believe, something new in this kind of poetry.

Haiku PUNchlines owe a few ideas and suggestions to Sylvia Rubin, Bernie Gutstadt, Chuck Farber, and Jackie Treatman. I am especially grateful to Ed Cichorek for suggesting the title of my previous tome, Haiku PUNmanship.

Dedication

To Abbe Jo and Jeffrey, Scott and Linda, Melissa and Bryon, Jennifer and Anthony;

Elexa, Ava, Jake, Troy and Anthony Jackson and any more great-grandchildren to come,

And

To the cherished memory of

Elaine Treatman, who started it all

Foreword

The haiku is a very old Japanese verse form that expresses cogently a thought in an economical three lines, five syllables in lines 1 and 3, seven syllables in line 2. In this book, you will occasionally discover a line shortened or extended by a syllable. For this peccadillo, I plead poetic license.

In this book, as in my previous five, I have melded the haiku with the pun - a form of humor considered lowly by many. Not me, I have always loved and flung puns, especially when I wanted to get thrown out of parties that bored me.

All of these haikus are mine. Most of the embedded puns are mine. I wove puns into haikus, a shotgun marriage I pray will entertain you with giggles, groans, or both.

Paul Treatman

Smoked salmon mogul
Gives exec job with perx of
Lox, stock and Carole.

Hock shop posts a sign
Over jewelry display,
"Once Upon a Crime."

Hindi Women Clash
For pastrami and corned beef
At New Delhi store.

"Too much insulin?
Be careful! Want to have a
Brush with a coma?"

"Proctologist? Did
He treat his parents well?"
"He almost rectum."

Turkey jilted by mate,
Who gobbles, "I flew the coop
And not coming beak."

Gent in Chinatown
Poisons dish, almost victim
Of chop sueycide.

Contentious couple
Standing before the judge and
Smirking snide by snide.

Did that Irish gent
Give his colleen a diamond
Ring or a sham rock?

Convicts on death row
Still appeal to read the pen's
Daily Noosepaper.

With spinal column
Pain, gent seeks Chinese doctor
For backupuncture.

Exotic jungle
Bird and mate say they do what
Any toucan do.

Soprano sings song,
"God Bless America" from
C to shining C.

Most births are head first;
However, we know that some
Births are fetal first.

Jilted mechanic
Suffers from lost love,
Survives wrenching life.

"Don't you know, lover boy,
That I am inscrutable
And impregnable?"

"Are you not worried
You son is robbing people?" "As
Long as he stays stealthy."

Owl and pussycat
Went to sea, pussy drowned, owl
Didn't give a hoot.

Kid pushes ailing
Mule to vet, saying, "Doc, there is
This pain in my ass."

"Selling your poultry
Farm? Surprise when chickens
All come home to roast!

"She talks tough to me."
"Then ask for sympathy and
I find heart of cold."

Man pulled overboard
By blue marlin, alive
With reel recovery.

WaWa coffee, dude
Bars up to close-in counters
Of the third grind.

Boss screamed noisily
At employees, none knowing
What his temperament.

Musician goes to
Try out for symphony and
Could not reach first bass.

Off to church on week
Nights, when she expects to win
A lotto money.

Who is the killer?
Mystery writer keeps us
All in suspenders.

All this discussion
About drilling for oil is
Becoming a bore.

Gun moll wants out, feels
Herself so trapped between a
Sock and a hard face.

"It is time for you
To use a good lotion for
After shave." "Musk I?"

Mechanic pours oil
Into engine, sees light at
End of the funnel.

His job at the dump
Is to destroy computers -
Internet hacking.

Mrs. Malaprop:
New church? I am soon to join
The conflagration.

Farmer blames his poor
Production of the lambs on the
Silence of his rams.

Poultry farmers plan
Ads, search for proper goose for
The propaganda.

Condom maker boasts
Huge profits at year's end, but
He stretches the point.

The famished chowhound
Gobbled up his potatoes
From starch to finish.

Kermit the Frog jumps
Into pond, hits head on the
Rocks and almost croaks.

Prospector strikes gold,
Runs into office tripping and
Falls on his assay.

Booklet prepared for
Mucinex users called "Great
Expectorations."

In burger eating
Contest, gent swallowed fast, yet
Could not ketchup.

Olympic swimmer,
Vegan, patiently waited
For time to endive.

The guide misled the
Group of tourists, so a few
Left detour angry.

Admirers pursued
Reluctant virgin until
She was chaste no more.

British convert to
Buddhism chooses noon for
Changing of the God.

"Like my new dining
Room?" "Yes, but now let's go and
Check your living womb."

"Let's make a thirteenth
Baby." "Fine, just give me one
More fecund," she says.

Royal wedding was
One more occasion for rounds
Of tea and trumpets.

Mrs. Malaprop:
"Have an itch? Then rub it with
Calcimine lotion."

Politician's speech
Frightens the audience with
A sudden bombast.

Roofer recovers
From chicken pox, then returns
To work with shingles.

Actress rehearses
Hospital drama, cannot
Read the doctor's script.

Auto maker claims
His electric models to
Be strong and fuelproof.

Bullfighter shops at
Home depot for new home, seeks
Help to picador.

Pardoned so soon from jail,
He was grateful being just
A flash in the pen.

Man to wife at meal:
If at first you don't succeed,
Then fry, fry again.

Stage frightened actress
Prays she can overcome this
Case of a tension.

To William Shakespeare,
Sir: How much do I love thee?
Let me count the plays.

Doc to Rabbi: "How's
Your leg" Rabbi: "With a cane
I can be able."

Processor of swine
Joins clothier to launch a
Lard and Taylor.

Returning from blood
Bank, honeymooners want to
Display sign, "Just Bled."

Husband learns his wife
Pregnant again, finds her to
Be overbearing.

The recovery of the
Ill child had been a happy
Case of touch and grow.

Geezers on fiber
Diet play boweling game
On daily basis.

Magellan was the
First old world explorer to
Circumcise the globe.

He flirted with the
Young beauty with those thoughts
Of attemptation.

She: "Are we not too
Tired for that?" He: "Of course not,
We have synergy."

Mrs. Malaprop:
If you walk downstairs, you must
Grab the barrister.

Droll orthopedist
Casts my fractured leg with his
Sense of humerus.

All the insects in
The meadow wanted to know
Just what kaydid.

Horseman-farmer champs
At the bit to take care of
The ants in his plants.

Boy and girl vegans
Go with expectation to
Woo in their mush room.

Mrs. Malaprop:
Each time eat I have a
Case of ingestion.

CEO swiftly
Takes steps to get rid of his
Board of Defectors.

Soprano hired to
Perform on a cruise ship and
Sing on the high C's.

A hungry swimmer
Wants to try currants
Before ocean plunge.

Bride and groom. Before
Altar, both with credit maxed:
"Till debt do us part."

When a snaggle-tooth
Old hag came on to me, zoom!
I ran for my wife!

Trembling wise guys soon
Agree to a new wetness
Protection program.

Architect has an
Obsession sometimes called
Edifice complex.

Musician moms who
Make preserves get together
For a jam session.

Wanting to purge his
Haunting memories, he drank
Milk of Amnesia.

College fencing team
Adopts a fighting battle
Cry: "En Garde We Thrust."

Mom: "Swear you'll never
Wet your pants again." "Cross my
Heart and hope to dry."

Find no pay phone in
Prison, convict asks warden:
Give me a cell phone?

Subaru salesman
Complains to spine doc
That he has out back.

U.S. Navy Seals
Gave bin Laden his final
Meal à la cartridge.

Sub sights enemy
Battleship and fires off a
Huge tornado.

"Chartered in the storm?"
"Our fishin'?-no good. We just were
Flounderin' around."

Guy rushes into
Incontinental Hotel
For rapid relief.

Lower East Side folks
Anxious to see "From Here
To Attorney Street."

Colonoscopy:
There's grief at the start but there's
Relief at the end.

Fist violin fails
To show for rehearsal, the
Fiddler on the goof.

Actresses star as
Shopaholics in new film,
"Sachs and the City."

The school kids go to Lunch: hysteria in the Cafeteria.

Before seven year
Itch, gent writes a book called "The
Best Years of My Wife."

To measure firearm
Action, you need to know some
Triggernometry.

Matricide fiend
Writes memoir, "I
Dismember Mama."

"Geez, dad. Please, no more
Alcohol." "Think I'll take that
With a grain of malt."

"Too much love making
Can wear us both out." That's how
The nooky crumbles.

Spiritualist:
"Neither rosy nor grim,
I'm your happy medium."

"That burlesque show we
Saw cost us cheap, you agree?"
"It was a ripoff."

Five months pregnancy,
Ecstatic to know she was
Expectorating.

"This manifest shows
The pier of debarkation."
"Eh, which dock you meant?"

Dancing With The Scars:
Fast old couple stumbles
Doing the quirk step.

About to wed, the
Couple joins lawyer at bar
To get a pre-nip.

Nasa hope to launch
Astronauts to Mars as soon
As they can planet.

Cannibalistic
Politics in Washington-
Elephant bites donkey.

Great duo, Fred and
Adele, famed years ago as
Dancing With Astaires.

That musician loves
Playing on the strings of his
Brand new mandible.

Mrs. Malaprop:
How that tramp gambles! She is
A real slut machine!

Hear about those two
Silkworms who had a race and
Ended in a tie?

Guy propositions
His date hoping to secure
Blanket approval.

Athlete leaves his flame
To complete in Olympics,
Still bearing the torch.

Moths invade closet
And munch for nights and days on
Serial coatmeal.

First the Arctic, then
Antarctic, adventurer
Becomes bipolar.

Executioner
Finally masters job and
Gets the hang of it.

"Believe me, doc, my
Foot still hurts." "I'll give you the
Benefit of the gout."

Dermatologist
Succeeds because he started
His practice from scratch.

Failed at every
Line of work because he was
A jerk of all trades.

Historians say
Nixon's resignation was
Unpresidented.

Lesbian partners
Upset when incontinence
Springs leak in the dyke.

Enthusiastic
Lumberjack begins to write
Prologue for memoirs.

Crooked lawyer dubbed
By outraged clients as their
Attorney-out-law.

Infectious disease
In ham can be a poorsign
In preparation.

Asteroid menace
Nearing Earth while scientists
Debate its gravity.

Helen of Troy hoped
Against hope, praying hard to
See Achilles heal.

You should see and hear
That rambunctious kid being
Fed peaches and scream.

Crowds on Black Friday
Turn all those stores with discounts
Into shopping mauls.

Hungry gigolo
Tasting summer sweet tart and
Juicy winter squash.

Mexican hooker
Calls to waiting room, "Easy now,
Just Juan at a time."

Elizabethan
Chef creates new dish -
The hamlet and yeggs.

Mouth wet with spittle,
Basketball star begins his
Dribbling on the court.

"Are you keeping that
Bird warm and comfy enough?"
"My polly Esther?"

Boss offers me a
Small cubicle; he has me
Over a carrel.

Walking around Rome,
Feet in agony, hope Pope
Will bless our poor soles.

That luxury car,
Six doors and six wheels, is the
Longest limo seen.

Full term pregnancy
Boards plane; hostess soon
Helps with the air-borne.

"Waiter, no dumpling
In my soup? I charge you with
Wanton negligence!"

Customer in the
Bakery tells rapping clerk,
"Get to rack and roll!"

Beautiful buffet,
Guests on diets crowd around
The veggie table.

A poolroom champion
Trying to rob a teller
With neat bank shot.

Liquor distiller
Near Antwerp produces new
Booze he calls Belle Gin.

"Did you ever meet
My significant udder?"
Asks the bull of his friends.

Hirsute gent likes to
Kiss the girls while brushing them
Off at the same time

"Any boarding now?"
"Sorry, all staterooms booked, not
One is vacant, see?"

Botched the barbeque,
Burnt the meats black, and I turned
Green around the grills.

Jurors start writing
Lunch choices when judge proclaims,
"Order in the court."

I hate to view films
About ghoulish things except
Once in a blue goon.

Slumlord released from
Jail decided to give tenants
A new lease on lice.

Mrs. Malaprop:
It gets very hot once you
Cross the Equation.

Sparring until the
Knockout punch, champ had the
Patience of a feint.

Godfather makes peace
With rivals and proclaims, "Let
Bye guns be buy guns."

Math major asks dad
To please cosine his college
Loan applications.

District attorney
Scares defense witnesses with
Trial and terror.

Twins: One follows the
Osteo path; the other
One, the psycho path.

Scotsman in the West
Village alters outfit, does
Not want to be kilt.

Rookie ball player
Purchased first home, realized
What his first base meant.

Judge Joe and Judge Joan
Meet and plan to wed after
One year of courtship.

She let the poodle
Bark at her, would not let the
Doberman pinscher.

Japanese warlords
Brandished swords in feudal days,
Too early to shoguns.

Ivory poachers
Return to Alabama
Where Tuscaloosa.

"Rabbi, could you rid
My kid of demons?" "I have
No rite to do that."

Two owners of bar
Say their partnership is like
Gin joint custody.

The felons in the
Lock-up enjoyed Halloween
With their prison gourds.

Home builder skimmed some
Materials because he
Wanted to gypsum.

Used the f-word so
Often during golf game he
Was par for the curse.

"I really didn't see
Nothin'.", Judge. "So suddenly
You're an eyewitless?"

"Jump from that diving
Board already, you know, the
Sooner the wetter."

Stop that hilarity
And screaming already and
Tighten those buccals!

She became irate
When her swim coach offered to
Show her the breast stroke.

Dermatologist tells
Patient that she must start to
Liquidate her skin.

Judge sends felon for
Psychiatric test, jurist
Was great at judge-mental.

Drunk grabs a cool beer
In February, sobs, "Please
Be my Ballentine."

Male boa never
Seeks mate, is this a case of
Reptile dysfunction?

Where the grassland meets
The desert, see a hut with
Sign, Custard's Last Stand.

Acupuncture of
Equine spine is sometimes applied
To avert a bray.

Kids failing college
Entrance commiserate
At bawling alley.

Mrs. Malaprop:
Will that thin, smart girl ever
Become fatuous?

Korean cleric
Weds one thousand couples, the
More the marrier.

From his rich digs in
London Town, he fled to her
Arms in Notting flat.

"No, doc, I want to
Sew my wound myself." "Then go
Ahead, suture self."

She wanted to kick
Me out at Christmas, but I
Dodged her missile toe.

Spraying on the worst
Perfume reflects a habit
Of wishful stinking.

Infatuated
With stunning actress, gent tweets
He plans to stork her.

Stone cutter suffered
So much financial pain that
He lost his marbles.

Going off to sea
Again, fisherman joins group
Who are musselbound.

He regarded the
Words from her tender trap a
Bid to tend her trap.

Songstress buys cloth
The seamstress needs to fashion
For her new pinafore.

Fishermen compete
Hooking worms fast, winner is
The master baiter.

Storage holes in ground,
Farmers waited for months for
Their stashed potatoes.

Sailor also works
In mountain climber rescue,
Is called fissure man.

"Yiddish Mikado"
Operetta parody, -
Gilbert and Solomon's

Cryptorchid gent
Sees lawyer to prepare "Last
Will and Testicle."

Candy loving guy
In drag begins to enjoy
His new tootsie role.

Dowager had thought
That by her dotage she would
Have finished humping.

Obama's English
Grew from tutorials at
College speakeasies.

Patient: "I dream of
Tepee and of wigwams." Doc:
"Your dreams are intense."

Geometrician
Loves to fish because he is
An expert angler.

Mrs. Malaprop:
"I'm happy to attend your
Wedding deception."

Overweight cleric
Calls physical trainer for
An abs solution.

Title of movie
About serial killer:
"Fatal Subtraction."

Latin musician
Tries fishing, fails to cast a
Line or castanet.

Wall Street millionaire
Buy's Rocky's gym and calls it
My New Sock Exchange.

First they wrote e-mails
Then they posted on facebook,
Now they are tweethearts.

Wily thief strolled through
Market aisles, stopped at produce,
Snatched pears with aplomb.

Two TV chefs plan
To co-author memoir, "The
Bear Years of Our Knives."

Before the wedding,
Dad spent many thousands of
Bucks on my torso.

Family starts road
Trip to nudist camp as kid
Shouts, "Are we bare yet?"

Cutlery Shop clerk;
"Merry Christmas to all, and
To all a good knife."

"What did her test of
Character reveal?" "As I
Thought, she scored the mean."

About the Author

He lived his early years in New York City.

His formal education includes Bachelor of Arts, Master of Arts and Doctor of Philosophy degrees.

He was a decorated combat medic in World War II.

He was a teacher, school principal and school superintendent.

He acted in community theater and film.

He currently resides in a New Jersey adult retirement community, active in local and veterans' affairs.

He has two children, four grandchildren and five great grandchildren.

He is at peace with himself and wishes peace for all mankind.

2012

Encomiums

In a short time... you taught me more about teaching than I learned in four years of college...

A neophyte teacher

...You could solve problems because you were able to anticipate them before they could occur...

A professional colleague...

...Educator of the Year...

Doctorate Association of NYC Educators

...You're too much...

A reader of author's haikus for punsters

...Excellent service in behalf of veterans...

The American Legion

...Lifetime achievement... Who's Who in America...Who's Who in the World...

President/CEO, Marquis Who's Who

...In face of hostile fire...You courageously assisted in the evacuation of numerous wounded men to an aid station...Bronze Star Medal for valor...

First U.S. Infantry Division

...Chevalier in the French Legion of Honor...

President of the Republic of France

Afterword

Dear Reader:

Giggles and groans, I hope you enjoyed these silly Haiku PUNchlines. Until I create book number 7 (may I live that long!), I leave you with this admonition:

Revise this haiku

And you'll be arrested for

Disturbing the piece.

Peace and love,
The Author
2012